P9-CSG-402

CHICKEN SOUP FOR THE SOUL® CARTOONS FOR MOMS

Jack Canfield
Mark Victor Hansen
John McPherson
Creator of *Close to Home*

Health Communications, Inc.
Deerfield Beach, Florida

www.hci-online.com
www.chickensoup.com

CLOSE TO HOME ©2003 *John McPherson. Reprinted with permission of Universal Press Syndicate.*
www.ucomics.com.

For information on reprinting any cartoons in this book, please go to *www.amureprints.com.*

Library of Congress Cataloging-in-Publication Data

McPherson, John, date.
    Chicken soup for the soul : cartoons for moms / Jack Canfield, Mark Victor
Hansen, [cartoons by] John McPherson.
      p. cm.
     ISBN 0-7573-0087-1
    1. Motherhood—Caricatures and cartoons.   2. Mothers—Caricatures and
cartoons.   3. American wit and humor, Pictorial.   I. Hansen, Mark Victor.
II. Canfield, Jack, date.   III. Title.

  NC1429.M275A4 2003
  741.5'973—dc21

                            2003040706

©2003 Jack Canfield and Mark Victor Hansen
ISBN 0-7573-0087-1

All rights reserved. Printed in the United States of America. No part of this publication
may be reproduced, stored in a retrieval system or transmitted in any form or by any
means, electronic, mechanical, photocopying, recording or otherwise, without the writ-
ten permission of the publisher.

HCI, its Logos and Marks are trademarks of Health Communications, Inc.

Publisher: Health Communications, Inc.
          3201 S.W. 15th Street
          Deerfield Beach, Florida 33442-8190

Cover design by Larissa Hise Henoch
Inside formatting by Anthony Clausi

With love, for all moms everywhere.
—Jack Canfield and Mark Victor Hansen

For mom, you're the greatest!
—John McPherson

Other books by John McPherson

Close to Home
Dangerously Close to Home
One Step Closer to Home
The Silence of the Lamberts
Close to Home Revisited
Home: The Final Frontier
Close to Home Unplugged
Striking Close to Home
The Close to Home Survival Guide
The Get Well Book
High School Isn't Pretty
Close to Home Uncut
The Scourge of Vinyl Car Seats
Close to Home Exposed
The Honeymoon Is Over

Contents

Acknowledgments

We wish to express our heartfelt gratitude to the following people who helped make this book possible:

Our publisher, Peter Vegso, for his vision and commitment to bringing *Chicken Soup for the Soul* to the world.

Patty Aubery, for being there on every step of the journey, with love, laughter and endless creativity.

Nancy Autio, Barbara LoMonaco, Veronica Romero, Inga Canfield, and Travis and Riley Mahoney, for helping with the final selection of cartoons.

Kathy Brennan-Thompson, for spearheading this project throughout the various phases of its completion.

Maria Nickless and Stephanie Thatcher, for their enthusiastic marketing and public-relations support and brilliant sense of direction.

Patty Hansen, for her thorough and competent handling of the legal and licensing aspects of the *Chicken Soup for the Soul* books. You are magnificent at the challenge!

Laurie Hartman, for being a precious guardian of the *Chicken Soup* brand.

Jesse Ianniello, for her dedicated service in helping to create this book.

Lisa Drucker and Susan Tobias, our editors at Health Communications, Inc., for their devotion to excellence.

Terry Burke and the marketing and public-relations departments at Health Communications, Inc., for doing such an incredible job supporting our books.

The art department at Health Communications, Inc., for their talent, creativity and unrelenting patience in producing book covers and inside designs that capture the essence of *Chicken Soup*: Larissa Hise Henoch, Lawna Patterson Oldfield, Andrea Perrine Brower, Lisa Camp, Anthony Clausi and Dawn Grove.

To Greg Melvin, Lee Salem and the other great folks at Universal Press Syndicate for their ongoing support of John and his work.

Special thanks to John Vivona and the Universal Press sales force for their hard work on John's behalf. You guys are the best.

Lastly, thanks to Chris Millis, John's right-hand man.

We are truly grateful and love you all!

Introduction

In today's high-pressured, fast-paced and hectic world, comedy and humor can help us step out of the routine of our daily lives, laugh at ourselves and our foibles, gain new perspective, and return to the challenges with a renewed sense of lightness and joy.

No role is more important in life than that of a mother. At the same time, no role demands more from an individual than the role of mother in today's world. Called upon to be nurturer, cook, counselor, mediator, advocate, chauffeur, nurse—and often the sole provider—the stresses are great, the challenges are strenuous, and the demands are never-ending. But, in the long run, the rewards are both immeasurable and enduring.

We hope that this lighthearted look at the lives of mothers—from conception, through the toddler and high-school years, to dealing with empty-nest syndrome—will provide you with many laughs, chuckles and smiles. Take a moment, step back and see the humor inherent in the demands of everyday life. Most importantly, remember not to take it all too seriously!

This collection of cartoons is a new venture for us at *Chicken Soup for the Soul*. We are excited to be teaming up with John McPherson, whose *Close to Home* cartoons have added humor to a number of *Chicken Soup for the Soul* titles over the years.

Since this is a new kind of book for us, we are eager to get your feedback on how you viewed this project. Please share your reaction by contacting us at:

Chicken Soup for the Soul
Cartoons for Moms
P.O. Box 30880
Santa Barbara, CA 93130

webmaster@chickensoupforthesoul.com

$\overline{1}$

IN THE BEGINNING

I don't know why they say, "You have a baby." The baby has you.

Gallagher

"Right now the baby is not in the proper position for delivery,
but I'm confident it will shift in time for your due date."

"Pssst! Carol! I'll split the office pool with you if
you'll induce labor on the 17th, 10 A.M."

". . . and over HERE you can see the SIXTH baby's head!
. . . Just kidding! There are only five babies."

"Trust me on this. If we want the dog to bond with the baby right away, he needs to eat all of his meals off your stomach during the third trimester."

"Well, I'd like to see the section in your health book
that says pregnant women shouldn't cook!"

"I want to start getting used to this backpack
before the baby comes along."

"There! You felt it kick *that* time, didn't you?"

"I had T-shirts made up with the baby's ultrasound on them!
I thought you could wear yours to your basketball league!"

With Skip adamant that they not find out the sex of their baby, Rita had secretly arranged for the sonogram technician to give her a coded signal.

Budget ultrasound.

"The baby just said, 'Don't even *think* of naming me Trevor!'"

"If you're planning on videotaping the birth, we're gonna need twenty minutes to touch up our makeup."

"We like to to try all our options before using drugs to induce labor."

"My, Helen, that certainly was a strong contraction!"

"I admire your interest in natural childbirth, but you've gotta be glad we talked you into having that epidural!"

"The maternity nurse let me borrow the other eight. I just want to see the look on my mother's face when she walks through the door."

"Serenity Noelle! The name we want on the
birth certificate is Serenity Noelle Wagner!
Write it down! *Write it down, I said!*"

Thanks to some virtually invisible fishing line, Nurse Kretchner was able to evoke some priceless facial expressions from proud parents and grandparents.

"Oh, wow! It's a birth announcement from the Fulkersons!
They just had twin boys!"

2

BABY, OH BABY

*Families with babies and families without babies are
sorry for each other.*

E.W. Howe

"She's a little cranky when she's tired."

"But hey, if you're not concerned about the threat of flash flooding and aren't 100 percent committed to your baby's safety, then maybe an amphibious stroller isn't for you."

"The doctor says she'll grow into her tongue."

"I worked out a deal with the woman in the apartment next door. She handles all of Jason's diaper changes for a buck a pop."

"Next I want you to hold your doll with one hand and then lightly rub a piece of beef on the pull tab of the diaper."

"My! What a good burp *that* was! Let's have one more now."

The latest in child-care products: fortune diapers.

On her flight from New York to Paris,
Paula falls victim to a diaper scalper.

"Okay! Cover me!"

Common parenting nightmares.

Seventy-two percent of all infants carry the anti-car seat gene,
allowing their stiffened bodies to resist forces in
excess of 100 pounds per square inch.

"Really? I'll have to try that. Could I have your name and address? My lawyer suggests that I keep a list of everyone who gives me unsolicited advice just in case there's a problem."

"He learned how to climb out, so we greased the crib."

3

TALES FROM TODDLERHOOD

*A*ny woman who can cope with the terrible twos can cope with anything.

Judith Clabes

"I tell ya, Helen, I'll sure be glad when the terrible twos are over."

Until the toddler years are well behind them, many
parents opt for the new disposable houses.

". . . spare diaper, ma'am? Stage three or stage
four? Bless you ma'am. Spare diaper?
Spare diaper, sir?"

"So far, five diaper services have canceled us."

"Now, now, sweetie. That was an *outdoor* voice.
We need to remember to use our *indoor*
voices when we're inside."

"It took some getting used to, but the kids love it.
Plus, I don't have to vacuum anymore."

"Well, there's a good one to know about. 'Stereo . . . receiver . . . needs . . . to be . . . moved up . . . higher.'"

How to toddler-proof your home.

"Isn't that pop-up book just the cutest thing?"

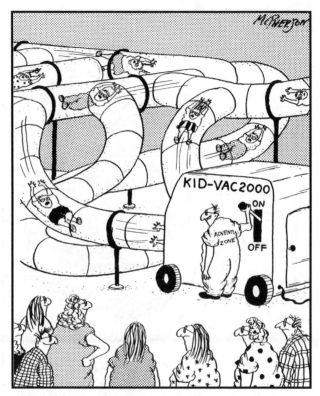

Closing time at Adventure Zone Playland.

"I'm concerned about his thumbsucking."

"All right now, give Mommy the super-glue."

"Okay, young man, that does it! When we get
home you are having a time-out!"

Thanks to her Early Tantrum Warning Device, Cathy had ninety seconds to take evasive action.

An unwavering truth of grocery shopping with a toddler: Your child *will* throw a tantrum, and it will invariably happen when your minister, pediatrician and mother-in-law are walking by.

To help them cope, many stay-at-home moms are turning to the new life-size T. Berry Brazelton doll.

The latest innovation for parents of toddlers:
peel-away kitchen flooring.

"Wonderful. We spend $200 on toys and she plays with a shoe box for three days non-stop."

"Leave the kitty alone, dear."

Overwhelmed by the rigors of raising a three-year-old and ten-month-old twins, Kim unilaterally opts for zone coverage.

"That's exactly what he wants you to do, Al. Can't you see this is just a ploy to get attention? Don't give him the satisfaction of knowing that his behavior upsets you."

Using stimulus/response, the Nelsons hoped to discourage
Jeremy from engaging in dangerous activities as a teenager.

"Well, thank you, Beth Ann! I'll put this up on the refrigerator right now!"

"Ummm . . . just a minute, Mom!"

4

CHILD CARE AND BABY-SITTING

She never quite leaves her children at home, even when she doesn't take them along.

Margaret Culkin Banning

"Not only will I *never* baby-sit for you again, it's gonna
cost you a hundred bucks to keep me from squealing
to the other sitters about your kids!"

Tollbooth operator Zena Calhoun
stumbles onto a gold mine.

The latest trend in baby-sitting: surcharges.

"Yep, that's definitely Tina baby-sitting for the Winslows!
Those back-stabbers stole our sitter, knowing full well
that tonight is our anniversary!"

"You can come out now, Mrs. Ziffler. Ron caught Howie and locked him in his room. Say, if you're free Friday night, we'd love to have you baby-sit again."

"I'm tellin' ya, Louise, that's the only thing that keeps me from going insane on rainy days."

"Are you sure you checked out this place's references?"

The agony of enrolling your child in a
hyper-illness-sensitive day-care center.

Hoping to convince management to provide a day-care center, employees at Gormley Industries staged a whine-in.

"Here's twenty bucks. Let 'em keep riding until
we get out of the movies."

Though they hadn't even stepped inside yet, veteran real estate agent Clair Gelt knew the sale was in the bag.

"It pays out in tokens good for one hour of free baby-sitting."

"Knock it off, Carlos! Remember, we agreed that
Isabelle would choose her own day-care provider."

The staff at Happy Hearts Day Care had its own unique way of
penalizing parents who were late picking up their kids.

5
24/7

Women are expected to do twice as much work as men in half the time and for no credit. Fortunately, this isn't difficult.

Charlotte Whitton

"I'll give you a hundred bucks if you'll watch my kids for twenty minutes while I take a nap."

Working couple Phil and Liz Plethcart had
perfected the art of the 6 P.M. hand-off.

"My baby-sitter's got the flu."

For those mornings when all she could manage to
throw on was a ratty T-shirt and sweats, Nancy
relied on her Classy-Bus-Stop-Mom Facade.™

Carol makes a last-ditch effort to keep the kids
from missing the bus.

With four kids to shuttle to activities, Donna's
new kid-launcher saved her valuable
time throughout the day.

As a mother of three active teenagers, Marilyn Gilcrest relied on a professional dispatcher to help coordinate her day.

Thoroughly burned-out by shuttling her kids to
and from school activities, Shelley
makes a drastic move.

Before taking the kids to Burger Baron, Linda
wisely installed her new fast-food tarp.

"I'll take six hamburgers, four small fries, four Cokes,
and a hundred napkins."

"I've been cooking in bulk to save money. Just tell me how much spaghetti you want me to reel off."

Dinnertime for working parents is
reduced to its most basic form.

"There! Maybe *now* you three will remember to take your plates to the kitchen after dinner!"

"They're done! HA HA! *All* the school lunches are done for the next 186 days! No more getting up at 6 A.M.! No more messy sandwiches! No more. . . ."

6

THE WONDERFUL WORLD OF PARENTING

Remember, when they have a tantrum, don't have one of your own.

Judith Kuriensky

Burger Baron ups the ante in the lucrative kids' meal market.

Only a veteran mom can master the
art of hands-free stroller unfolding.

"You got any bright ideas how to get a peanut butter and jelly sandwich out of the VCR?"

"Here's part of an old cheeseburger, and I
think I can feel a couple more french fries."

"You've got Minivanitis, Mrs. Keppler, commonly known as Reaching Back to Retrieve Your Screaming Toddler's Juice Cup While Driving Syndrome."

"He does not have a discipline problem! He's just had a little too much sugar, that's all."

Mrs. Zanski's fifteen-minute slide presentation quickly
set the tone for her parent-teacher conference
with the Murdocks.

"Andy! Start rewrapping 'em now!
Mom and Dad just pulled in the driveway!"

"Uhh . . . Excuse me, ma'am, but you've . . . uh . . . taken my cart by mistake. I believe that's yours there."

"Ma'am, I've been appointed spokesperson for the other passengers. We're prepared to offer you $637.82 to take a later flight."

Tired of being chastised by their three-year-old for not knowing all the "Thomas the Tank Engine" characters, the Gertmans wisely invested in flash cards.

Having successfully completed her shopping without a major tantrum, Linda now had to run the harrowing gauntlet of toy and candy dispensers.

"He was twenty-nine, living in L.A. I came across this big musty box of baseball cards just cluttering up the house, so I tossed them. Today, they'd be worth $80,000."

Carol Wichowski's empty-nest syndrome
takes a turn for the worse.

As Todd entered his sophomore year of college,
his mother's empty-nest syndrome worsened.

"First, the 900-square-foot heated tree fort. Then the fully operational backyard planetarium. And now this. It's all a well-orchestrated plot to make us look like the world's lousiest parents."

Like many parents, the Gelmans found themselves caught in a cycle of trying to outdo the previous year's birthday party.

$\overline{7}$

MARRIED WITH CHILDREN

Insanity is hereditary. You can get it from your children.

Sam Levenson

"I calculated that by the year 2012, we will have spent $78,760 for their allowances."

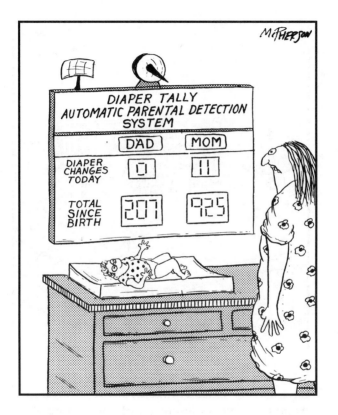

"Here's an interesting piece of trivia. Since the
baby was born, I've had 957 hours of sleep.
You've had 1,429."

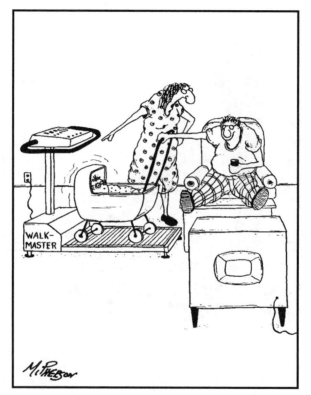

"This is *not* what I had in mind when I asked you to take the baby for a stroll."

"Oh, that? I thought I told you. *Dateline NBC* is going to feature us in a segment titled 'Working Couples: Who Does the Brunt of the Housework?'"

"Bud's Garage is seven miles ahead. 'Two stars. Great soap dispensers, attractive tilework. But toilet paper supply is unreliable and flies can be horrible.'"

"Isn't there a snooze button somewhere on him that we can hit?"

The latest in specialty parenting magazines.

"Are you the genius who left a bag of lollipops in the backpack?"

"It was the cutest thing! Jordan felt so bad about leaving his marbles on the stairs, he made this cast for his dad out of Legos!"

"Gene, e-mail the kids and tell them to come downstairs for dinner."

"Aunt Delia! Uncle Buzz! How nice of you to stop by unexpectedly! Unfortunately, we've got the measles! Can you believe it? All of us!"

"Okay! Who's the wise guy who put the Mr. Yuk
sticker on my turnip casserole?!"

"I'll be there in a second, dear. I'm tucking the kids in."

"Anytime one of the kids gets an illness we cross it off. When we complete a row, Ed and I are going to Tahiti for three weeks."

"Okay, Mr. Cynic! Twenty-two years and four kids later, it still fits! Pay up!"

At last, help for parents who rarely get a
chance to talk to each other.

"With five kids in the house, this was the only way we could think of to give everybody a fair shot at the bathroom."

8

THE TEENAGE YEARS

It is simply wonderful to have children, whether they are toddlers or grown women and men on their own. When they are teenagers, however, sometimes you wish you could cancel the whole deal.

Nicki Mutter

As parents of three teenage girls, the Nardleys
were having hours of fun with their
new Embarrass-o-Meter.

"Mrs. Cradner, I'm afraid that, due to excessive use, the earpiece has grafted itself to your daughter's head."

"I can't believe you cleaned up your entire
room in five minutes."

"You just said I had to clean my room. You didn't say I couldn't use my allowance to pay someone else to do it."

"Well, I don't believe it! Your room is spotless! And in just ten minutes! Hey, wait a second . . . where's your rug?!"

Danny's mom stumbles onto his
undesirable-food disposal system.

"Kevin, we've been telling you for years, 'Eat your
vegetables or the Vegetable Police will get you!'
You thought it was just a big joke, ha, ha, ha."

"THERE! I cleaned up my plate. NOW
may I be excused?"

"I do *not* want you feeding the dog scraps at the dinner table!"

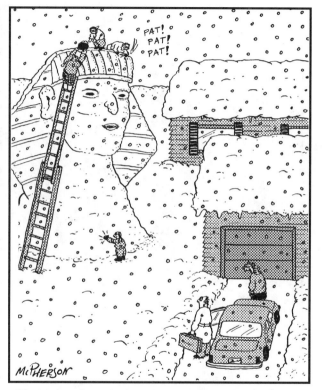

"Amazing how industrious they can be when
the Nintendo is broken, isn't it?"

"Aw, come on, Mom. We worked
on it all afternoon."

"Okay, when Mom comes out to get the
mail, grab her as hard as you can!"

"Check it out, Mom! We're having a snowball fight
with three kids in Syracuse!"

"Whatever you do, don't tell Mom he's here."

"Sorry, Mom. I thought I had enough
momentum to clear the house."

"Tommy? He's upstairs in his room having 'time out.'"

"Well, thank you, Wayne and Elwin. An Assault of the Psycho Slime Monsters Nintendo cartridge. How thoughtful of you."

"For heaven's sake, you're right! His hands have actually grafted themselves onto the surface of the Playstation™ controls!"

"Okay, Mom and Dad are watching TV. Stash the box in the bushes,
and let's sit down across from them like nothing is up."

"*Another* 'Fantastic'?! Danny you have *really* turned
your grades around! I am so proud of you!"

"You guys didn't happen to see my science project
come crawling through here, did you?"

"Eh, eh, eh! You know the rules!
No bugging Mom at work!"

"Okay, Bobby! You can open your eyes now!"

9

PROUD PARENTS

A mother is neither cocky nor proud because she knows the school principal may call at any minute to report that her child has just driven a motorcycle through the gymnasium.

Mary Kay Blakely

Prenatal peer pressure.

"We've already had calls from two pro soccer teams and an international water skiing show."

"Really? Three weeks? Brandon started sleeping twelve
hours at just two weeks, which made it a lot easier
for me to get back into my step aerobics class!"

"We've already had endorsement offers
from three shampoo companies."

The Mendricks began showcasing their son's talents
long before he was even born.

"Yep, this is definitely a record! 139 inches! It beats the creamed corn back on Aug. 14 by 6½ inches."

"Stan, will you knock it off!
He will walk when he's ready to walk!"

"Ryan's walking two months earlier than most other kids, thanks to these training shoes that Gary made in the basement."

"Their four-year-old just got potty-trained."

"We were running out of room for the kids' drawings so we had to get another refrigerator."

"And over here we have Tyler's 'Blue Period.'
Notice the strong, sweeping strokes that
seem to leap right off the canvas."

"Two or three months ago I was always exhausted because he needed constant attention. Now that he's able to entertain himself, life is *so* much easier."

With her fifteen-month-old still not walking, Brenda
felt a subtle competition building between her
son and the Wilsons' nine-month-old.

The minimum age requirement for competitive
youth sports continues its downward spiral.

When soccer moms go too far.

10

CREATIVE PARENTING

Raising children is a creative endeavor, an art, rather than a science.

Bruno Bettelheim

"This playpen is good up to age fourteen!"

"Don found a way to wire the baby monitor
into the stereo."

For those really frantic diaper changes,
Rita relied on her foot-activated wipes dispenser.

"It's a thirty-day diaper. When he needs a change, just turn the handle on the hermetically sealed diaper canister, and . . . VOILÀ!"

Thanks to Zach's new hydraulic pants,
Linda no longer had to worry about whether
a high chair was available.

"I thought of getting a backpack, but they cost a fortune, so I just made outfits for me and Leon out of Velcro and voilà!"

"Believe me, we tried everything to soothe her colic. Car rides, massage, yoga, mud baths. Then one day, out of desperation . . ."

"Dan backed over the stroller in the driveway."

"Bill's away for two weeks, and he made me
swear not to let the baby take her first steps
until he's home to see the big event."

An essential parenting skill: speeding up
bedtime by condensing children's books.

Advanced parenting techniques.

Using technology to allay your child's fears.

Saving herself hours of cleanup time, Carol wisely
outfitted Justin with a personal toy rake.

As soon as the Excessive Trashiness Alarm™
sounded in his room, Matt knew he was in big trouble.

"Really, I'm serious. I'm talking to you from a phone booth in the living room. It's the only way I can talk on the phone without being harassed."

"To discourage anybody from shaking the gifts, one of those boxes has been filled with hornets. Yep, I hate to think what those hornets might do if anybody shook their box."

"For once I wish she'd just say 'You're grounded!'
and be done with it."

"It's called 'Sounds of the Dentist's Office.' Dr. Millis recommends we play it for an hour every day to encourage all of us to brush and floss."

"This way the kids think twice before they
come charging into the kitchen!"

"We teach the neighborhood kids we like how to get through the maze. Those who annoy us can get lost in here for hours until they just leave."

"I've got the thing wired up to a generator in the basement.
We cut our electric bill in half last year."

"With the kids tromping in and out in this messy weather,
the electric doormat has been a godsend."

"Hey, I've had it with getting them in and out of winter clothes. This new flexible foam insulation goes on quickly and peels right off."

Emily's new Bus Stop Prop™ allowed her to
catch some desperately needed additional sleep.

As a service to mothers, school buses at
Douglasville School District were outfitted
with forgotten-item retrieval bins.

"So I said, 'I don't care if it's an $800 option. I want the
shatter-resistant, soundproof barrier.'"

With cold and flu season in high gear, Brenda wisely carried her sneeze shield whenever she went out in public.

At the Mayfield Mothers Group weekly
Flintstones Vitamins trading session.

Having discovered that she's out of pasta and with dinner guests arriving in twenty minutes, Jean is forced to use the kids' macaroni necklaces.

"Isn't it clever? The legs pop out
when it's done cooking!"

"I made these out of leftovers from Thanksgiving
dinner. They're gravy Popsicles."

"It's your choice, kids."

In a technological breakthrough that would stun
the world, a leading auto manufacturer develops
a car that runs on kids' meal toys.

"Now what have I told you? *Never* bother Mommy
when she's in the bathroom!"

". . . and when it's time for you to buy new sneakers, the *least* expensive pair will be the ones you want. Any other pair will seem laughable by comparison . . ."

Supporting Others

In the spirit of fostering more love in the world, *Chicken Soup for the Soul* has made it a tradition to donate a portion of the net profits from every book title to a chosen charity. A portion of the proceeds from this book will be given to the **Saratoga County Economic Opportunity Council (EOC).**

A nonprofit food program, Saratoga EOC provides aid to low- and/or fixed-income people and families in crisis. Their means of aid include outreach, advocacy, a six-day-a-week food pantry and summer youth lunch programs. They help more than 15,000 individuals a year.

You may contact this organization at:

Saratoga County Economic Opportunity Council
P.O. Box 5120
Saratoga Springs, NY 12866
phone: 518-587-3158
e-mail: *sceoc@capital.net*

Who Is Jack Canfield?

Jack Canfield is one of America's leading experts in the development of human potential and personal effectiveness. He is both a dynamic, entertaining speaker and a highly sought-after trainer. Jack has a wonderful ability to inform and inspire audiences toward increased levels of self-esteem and peak performance.

He is the author and narrator of several bestselling audio- and video-cassette programs, including *Self-Esteem and Peak Performance, How to Build High Self-Esteem, Self-Esteem in the Classroom* and *Chicken Soup for the Soul— Live.* He is regularly seen on television shows such as *Good Morning America, 20/20* and *NBC Nightly News.* Jack has coauthored numerous books, including the *Chicken Soup for the Soul* series, *Dare to Win* and *The Aladdin Factor* (all with Mark Victor Hansen), *100 Ways to Build Self-Concept in the Classroom* (with Harold C. Wells), *Heart at Work* (with Jacqueline Miller) and *The Power of Focus* (with Les Hewitt and Mark Victor Hansen).

For further information about Jack's books, tapes and training programs, or to schedule him for a presentation, please contact:

Jack Canfield
P.O. Box 30880
Santa Barbara, CA 93130
phone: 805-563-2935 • fax: 805-563-2945
Web site: *www.chickensoup.com*

Who Is Mark Victor Hansen?

Mark Victor Hansen is a professional speaker who in the last twenty years has made over 4,000 presentations to more than 2 million people in thirty-two countries. His presentations cover sales excellence and strategies; personal empowerment and development; and how to triple your income and double your time off.

Mark has spent a lifetime dedicated to his mission of making a profound and positive difference in people's lives. Throughout his career, he has inspired hundreds of thousands of people to create a more powerful and purposeful future for themselves while stimulating the sale of billions of dollars worth of goods and services.

Mark is a prolific writer and has authored *Future Diary, How to Achieve Total Prosperity* and *The Miracle of Tithing*. He is coauthor of the *Chicken Soup for the Soul* series, Dare to Win and *The Aladdin Factor* (all with Jack Canfield), and *The Master Motivator* (with Joe Batten).

For further information about Mark, write:

MVH & Associates
P.O. Box 7665
Newport Beach, CA 92658
phone: 949-759-9304 or 800-433-2314
fax: 949-722-6912
Web site: *www.chickensoup.com*

Who Is John McPherson?

John McPherson was raised in a faraway place called Painted Post, New York. (We're not making this up.) He began cartooning at the age of four, with the bulk of his work appearing on walls, furniture and, at one point, a neighbor's dog. Most of this early work was poorly received. Discouraged, John turned his creative efforts to Play-Doh, pipe cleaners and Spirograph.

For the next fifteen years, John put his cartooning career on hold, until one day, during a very dull college engineering class, John drew a doodle in his notebook. His career was reborn. From that point in 1983, John began to draw voraciously despite the fact that his cartoons looked like he had drawn them using a pencil taped to his nose.

In the years that followed, John's cartoons appeared regularly in over forty magazines, and in 1992 Universal Press Syndicate and John teamed up to launch *Close to Home*. Since that time, *Close to Home* has earned its way into 700 papers worldwide, including *The Washington Post*, *Los Angeles Times*, *Tokyo Times* and *Hanoi Daily News*. In addition, John has published numerous book collections of his work, a yearly block calendar and an award-winning line of greeting cards with Recycled Paper Products.

In addition to his cartooning, John is an active speaker, talking to groups about the rigors of syndicated cartooning. He can be reached at *closetohome@compuserve.com*.

John lives in Saratoga Springs, New York, with his wife and two boys. When not drawing cartoons or playing with his kids, John spends time expanding his collection of soda-can pull tabs.

Making a Difference

Chicken Soup for the Soul Celebrates

T E A C H E R S

A Collection in Words and Photographs by
Jack Canfield & Mark Victor Hansen
and
Sharon J. Wohlmuth
Co-Creator of the *New York Times* Bestseller *Sisters*

Code #1045 • Hardcover • $12.95

Available wherever books are sold.
To order direct: Phone 800.441.5569 • Online www.hcibooks.com
Prices do not include shipping and handling. Your response code is CCS.

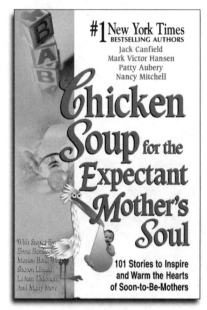

#1 New York Times
BESTSELLING AUTHORS
Jack Canfield
Mark Victor Hansen
Patty Aubery
Nancy Mitchell

Chicken Soup for the Expectant Mother's Soul

With Stories By:
Erma Bombeck
Marion Bond West
Sharon Linnéa
LeAnn Thieman
And Many More

101 Stories to Inspire and Warm the Hearts of Soon-to-Be-Mothers

Code #7966 • Paperback • $12.95

#1 New York Times
BESTSELLING AUTHORS
Jack Canfield
Mark Victor Hansen
Dorothy Firman
Julie Firman
Frances Firman Salorio

Chicken Soup for the Mother & Daughter Soul

With Stories By:
Joan Borysenko
Jacquelyn Mitchard
Eda LeShan
Laura Lagana
Patricia Lorenz

Stories to Warm the Heart and Honor the Relationship

Code #088X • Paperback • $12.95

Available wherever books are sold.
To order direct: Phone 800.441.5569 • Online www.hcibooks.com
Prices do not include shipping and handling. Your response code is CCS.